THIS WALKER BOOK BELONGS TO:

The author wishes to thank the following
for their help and co-operation:
TEREX • CASE POCLAIN • KRUPP INDUSTRIES •
SIMPLEX PILING • ORENSTEIN & KOPPEL •
JAMES HOWDEN • BLAW-KNOX • ATLAS LOADERS •
SCHWING/STETTER • TOWER DEMOLITION •
KOMATSU • NIPPON PNEUMATIC

First published 1991 by
Walker Books Ltd
87 Vauxhall Walk, London SE11 5HJ

This edition published 1992

Printed and bound in Hong Kong by
Sheck Wah Tong Printing Press Ltd

British Library Cataloguing in Publication Data
Radford, Derek
Building machines.
I. Title
428.6
ISBN 0-7445-2090-8

DEREK RADFORD

BUILDING MACHINES

AND WHAT THEY DO

WALKER BOOKS
LONDON

Drop-ball demolition
Whammmmm! Bang! Crash!
The drop-ball smashes into
an old building. It hits it
so that all the bricks go
crashing to the inside.

The crane
driver takes
aim.

cable

tipper lorry

Crusher demolition

A crusher is brought in to break up steel and concrete. The crusher bites, chews, twists and pulls at old buildings.

Pneumatic drills break up concrete.

This huge arm moves up and down.

RAT-A-TAT-TAT-TAT!

The driver controls all the actions.

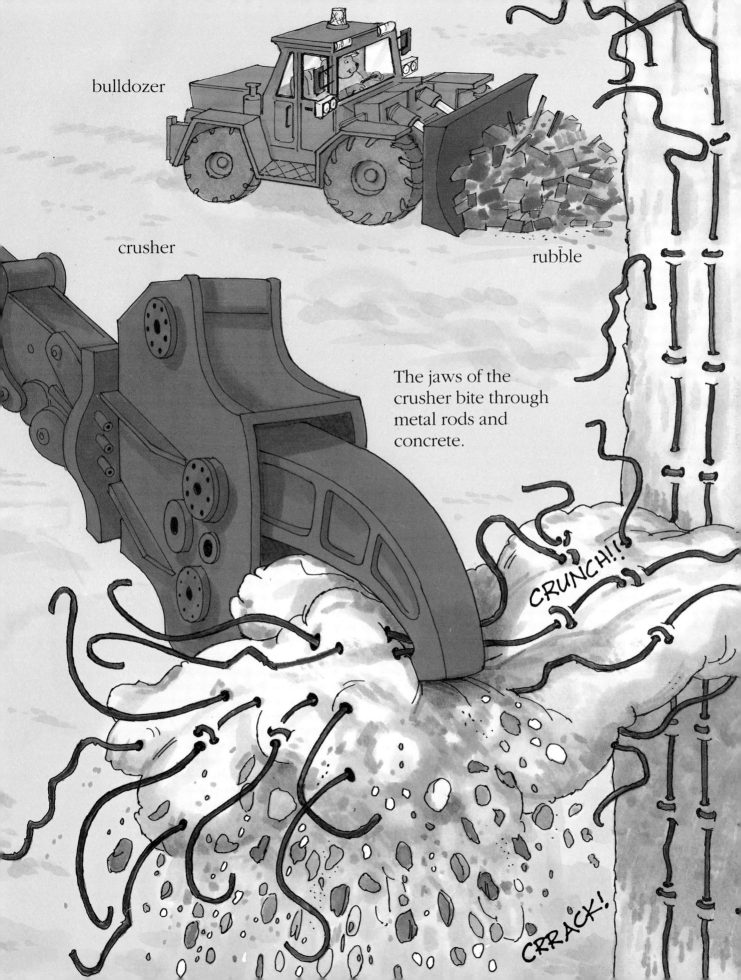

bulldozer

crusher

rubble

The jaws of the crusher bite through metal rods and concrete.

Site Clearing

Before a new building can be put up, there is a lot of work to do. The ground has to be levelled. Rocks and boulders have to be taken away.

Lorries take away broken-down boulders.

excavator

scoop

A hydraulic hammer breaks up rocks.

DAT-A-DAT-A-DAT-A-DAT!

electrical cables   skip   oil drums   planks   cement

SCREEEEECK

This scraper machine levels
the site by scraping a steel
plate over the ground.

The cab is
noisy and
vibrates a lot.

A dumper carries
loads of cement.

excavator

welding machinery

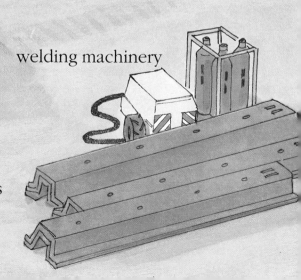

steel piles

Building site

The cranes are busy preparing the site for a big building. One is drilling holes for concrete supports. The other crane drives in strong steel piles.

oil drum

waste soil

drill

Markers show the crane driver where to drill.

Steel cages are put into the holes for extra strength.

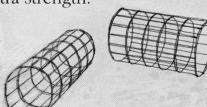

Concrete will be poured into these holes.

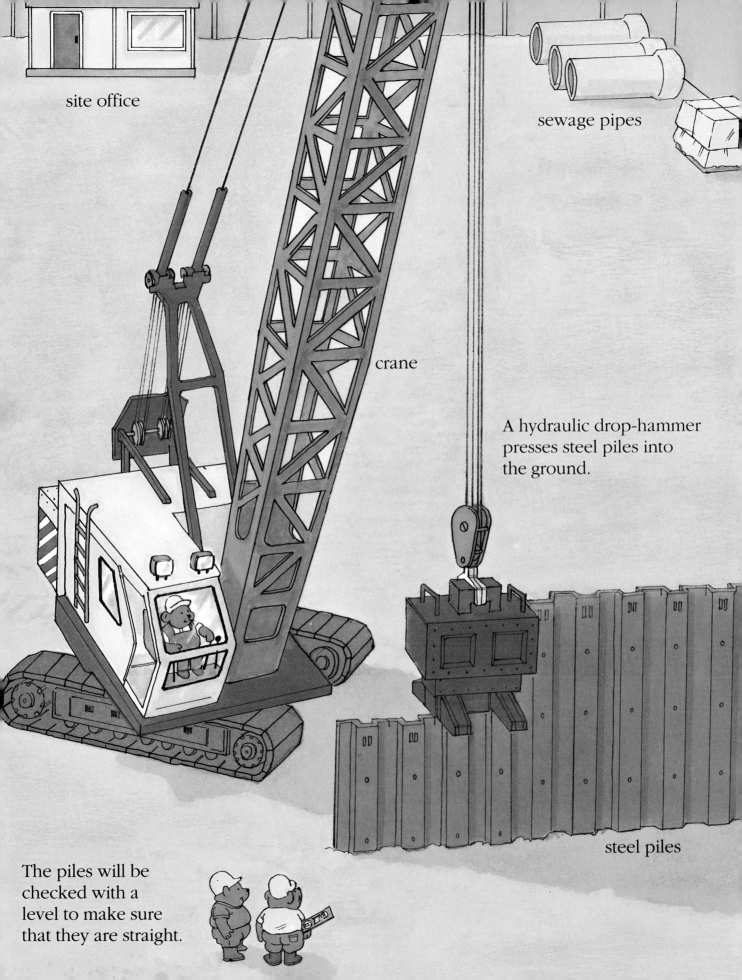

site office

sewage pipes

crane

A hydraulic drop-hammer presses steel piles into the ground.

steel piles

The piles will be checked with a level to make sure that they are straight.

Concrete mixer

Crrk! Crrk! Rrrurk! Stones, sand, cement and water are mixed up to make concrete. Then the mixer brings the concrete to the building site.

Sand, cement and stones go into the funnel.

The driver decides how much concrete to put in the dumper.

A dumper is like a big box on wheels.

SQUELCH

SQUIDGE

drum

water tank

Big blades
inside the
drum do the
mixing.

The truck has
a hose for
cleaning out
the mixer.

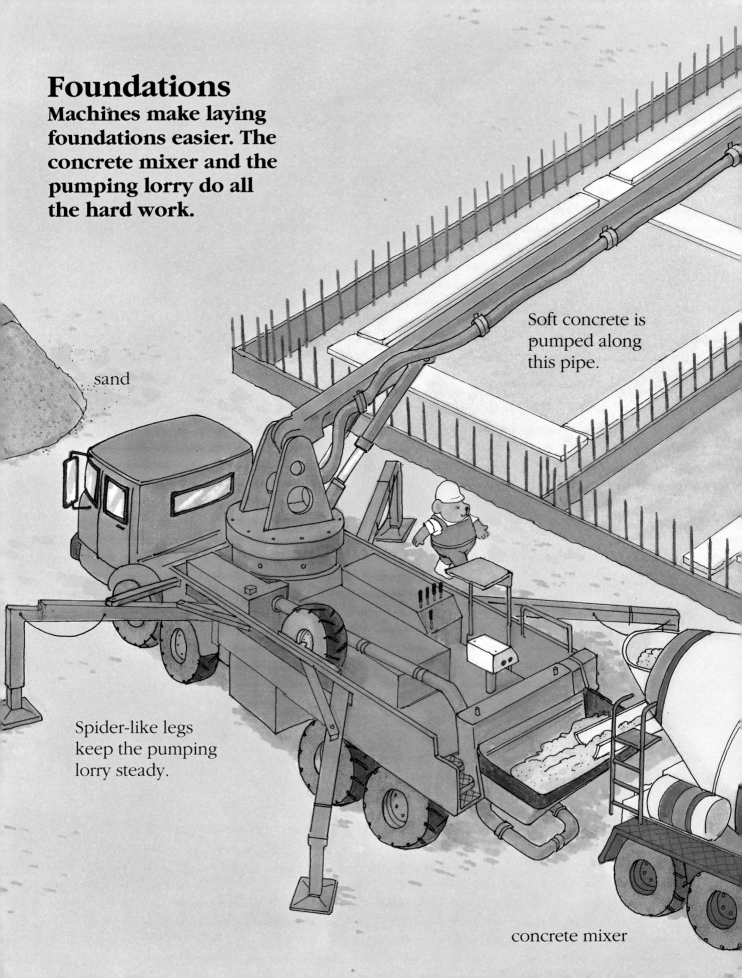

Foundations
Machines make laying foundations easier. The concrete mixer and the pumping lorry do all the hard work.

sand

Soft concrete is pumped along this pipe.

Spider-like legs keep the pumping lorry steady.

concrete mixer

Everyone walks on planks until the concrete sets.

The concrete is pumped by remote control.

The concrete goes into a bed of steel rods.

A vibrator presses the concrete down firmly.

SLOP GLUG

Unloading

Building materials such as bricks, concrete slabs or steel girders are very heavy. A mini crane that fits on a lorry makes unloading easier.

mini crane

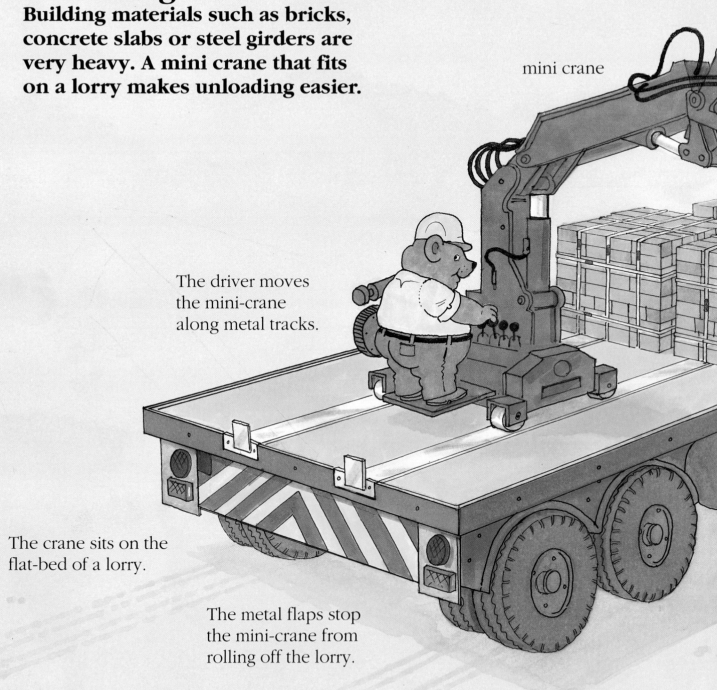

The driver moves the mini-crane along metal tracks.

The crane sits on the flat-bed of a lorry.

The metal flaps stop the mini-crane from rolling off the lorry.

The lifting crane grips
its load very tightly.

There are 1,536
bricks on this pallet.

Metal bands hold
the bricks together.

pallet is like a
ig wooden tray.

lifting prongs

fork-lift truck

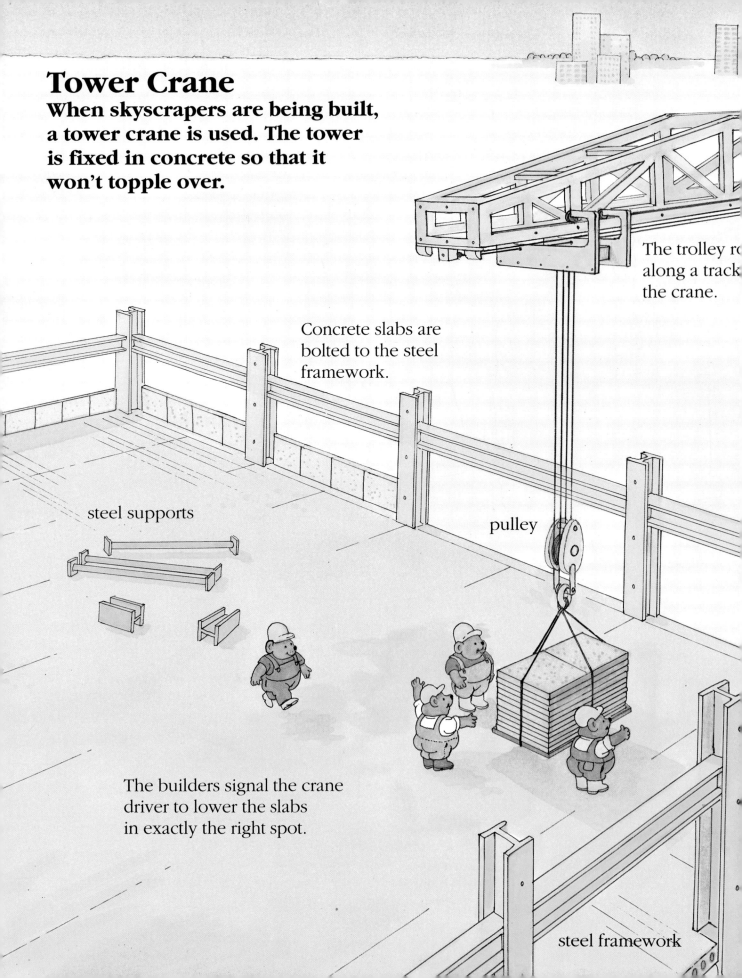

Tower Crane

When skyscrapers are being built, a tower crane is used. The tower is fixed in concrete so that it won't topple over.

The trolley r[o]
along a track
the crane.

Concrete slabs are
bolted to the steel
framework.

steel supports

pulley

The builders signal the crane
driver to lower the slabs
in exactly the right spot.

steel framework

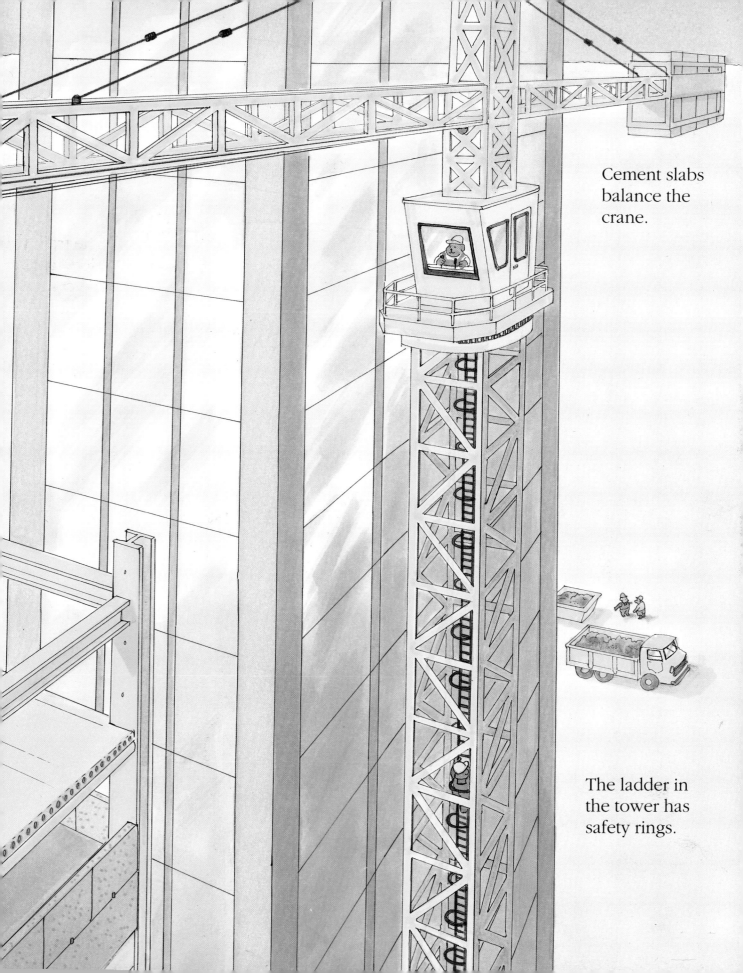

Cement slabs
balance the
crane.

The ladder in
the tower has
safety rings.

Excavation

This excavator fitted with a clam-shell bucket can fill a giant dump truck in one-and-a half minutes.

The jaws of the clam-shell bucket can open and close.

CRASH!
RUMBLE!

The foreman comes to check on progress.

This giant dump truck can carry up to 100 tonnes of stone.

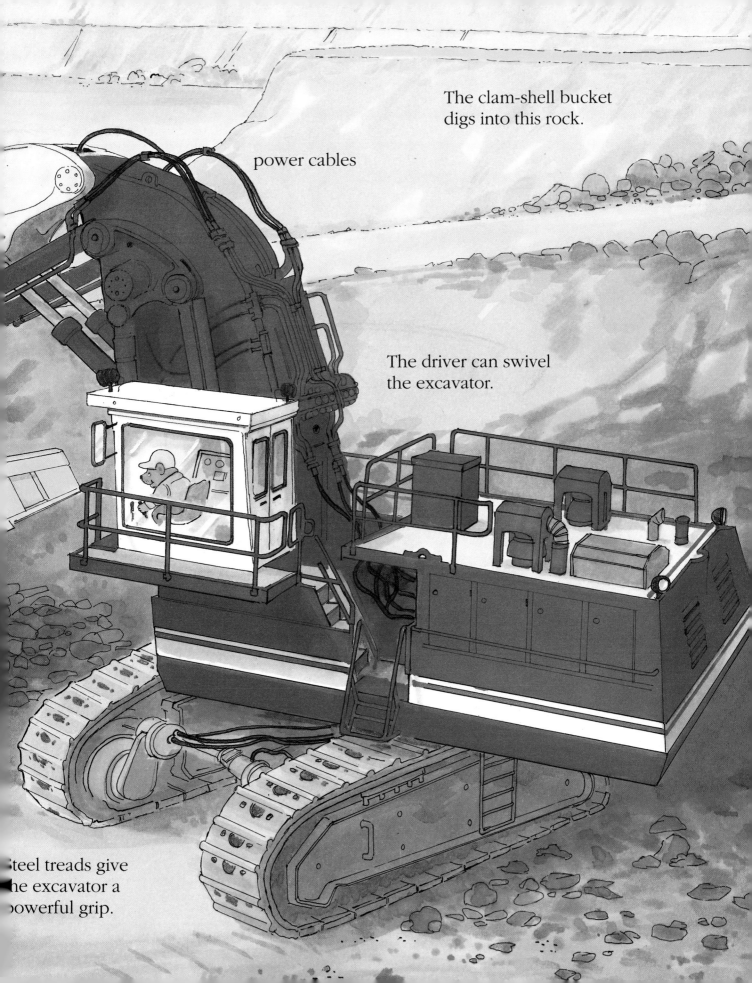

The clam-shell bucket
digs into this rock.

power cables

The driver can swivel
the excavator.

Steel treads give
the excavator a
powerful grip.

Road-making
Roads are made by laying hot tarmac on a foundation of broken stones. Tarmac sets hard when it is cold.

This is the engine of the road widener.

Someone directs the traffic.

GO

A road roller presses down the tarmac.

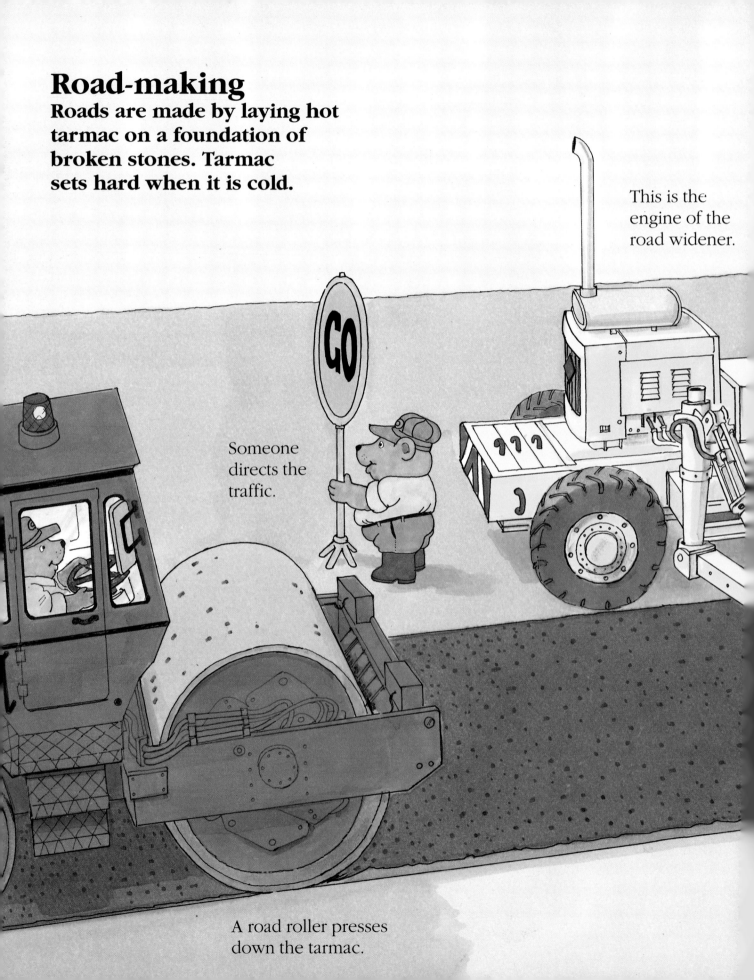

Tunnelling

This giant tunneller is like a mole working underground. The cut-away drawing shows how it tunnels through chalk.

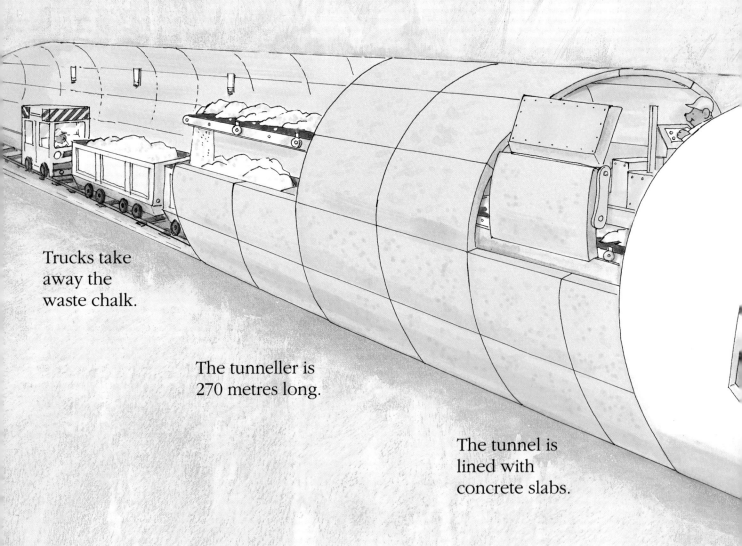

Trucks take away the waste chalk.

The tunneller is 270 metres long.

The tunnel is lined with concrete slabs.

Chalk is a soft soil.

computer operator
keps the tunneller
target.

There are more than
200 razor-sharp picks
on the cutting head.

conveyer belt
rries waste chalk.

Underwater bulldozer

Deep in the ocean, an underwater bulldozer
rips up rocks ready for bridge-building.
The bulldozer is lowered into the
water from a ship anchored
on the surface.

A cable shows
the ship above
where the
bulldozer is
working.

marker buo

This bulldozer is
60 metres under
the sea.

Fierce biades cut
into the rock.

A driver gives the bulldozer instructions by remote control.

BLIP BLIP BLIP BLIP

Messages from the ship can be sent via this receiver.

Crawler tracks keep the bulldozer steady.

scoop